Carrie Underwood

By Kylie Burns

Crabtree Publishing Company
www.crabtreebooks.com

Crabtree Publishing Company
www.crabtreebooks.com

Author: Kylie Burns
Publishing plan research and development:
Reagan Miller
Editors: Molly Aloian, Crystal Sikkens
Proofreader and indexer: Wendy Scavuzzo
Photo research: Crystal Sikkens
Designer: Ken Wright
Production coordinator and prepress technician: Ken Wright
Print coordinator: Margaret Amy Salter

Photographs:
Admedia: cover
Associated Press: pages 17, 18
Everett Collection: Kyle Cameron: page 14;
Mario Perez/©TriStar Pictures: page 24
Getty Images: Tony R. Phipps/WireImage:
page 6; Ray Mickshaw/WireImage: page 12;
Kevin Winter/Getty Images: page 13; Uri
Schanker: page 16; Kevin Mazur/WireImage:
page 19
Globe Photos, Inc.: John Barrett: page 8; Fitzroy
Barrett: page 10
Keystone Press: Photo by FOX Photo/
Entertainment Pictures: page 11; zumapress:
page 15; JM5/Wenn/Keystone Canada:
pages 20–21
Photoshot: page 7
Shutterstock: s_bukley: pages 1, 5 (top), 28; Mat
Hayward: pages 4, 25; Featureflash: page 5
(bottom); Dennis A. Crumrin: page 9; Phil
Stafford: page 22; Jaguar PS: pages 23, 27;
jkirsh: page 26

Library and Archives Canada Cataloguing in Publication

Burns, Kylie, author
    Carrie Underwood / Kylie Burns.

(Superstars!)
Includes index.
Issued in print and electronic formats.
ISBN 978-0-7787-0024-1 (bound).--ISBN 978-0-7787-0043-2
(pbk.).--ISBN 978-1-4271-9384-1 (pdf).--ISBN 978-1-4271-9378-0
(html)

        1. Underwood, Carrie, 1983- --Juvenile literature. 2. Singers-
-United States--Biography--Juvenile literature. 3. Country
musicians--United States--Biography--Juvenile literature. I. Title.
II. Series: Superstars! (St. Catharines, Ont.)

ML3930.U565B96 2013   j782.42164092   C2013-905221-6
                                                     C2013-905222-4

Library of Congress Cataloging-in-Publication Data

Burns, Kylie.
Carrie Underwood / Kylie Burns.
    pages cm. -- (Superstars!)
    Includes index.
    ISBN 978-0-7787-0024-1 (reinforced library binding) -- ISBN 978-
0-7787-0043-2 (pbk.) -- ISBN 978-1-4271-9384-1 (electronic pdf) --
ISBN 978-1-4271-9378-0 (electronic html)
    1. Underwood, Carrie, 1983---Juvenile literature. 2. Singers--
United States--Biography--Juvenile literature. I. Title.

ML3930.U53B87 2014
782.421642092--dc23
[B]

                                        2013030091

Crabtree Publishing Company

Printed in Canada/092013/BF20130815

www.crabtreebooks.com   1-800-387-7650

Published in Canada
Crabtree Publishing
616 Welland Ave.
St. Catharines, ON
L2M 5V6

Published in the United States
Crabtree Publishing
PMB 59051
350 Fifth Avenue, 59th Floor
New York, New York 10118

Published in the United Kingdom
Crabtree Publishing
Maritime House
Basin Road North, Hove
BN41 1WR

Published in Austral
Crabtree Publishing
3 Charles Street
Coburg North
VIC 3058

CONTENTS

Words that are defined in the glossary are in
bold type the first time they appear in the text.

Bursting Onto the Scene

The crowd chants loud enough to be heard backstage; "Carrie! Carrie! Carrie!" They grow more and more excited about the star's arrival. The lights go dim and a cheer explodes from the waiting fans as performing artist Carrie Underwood takes the stage at her very own concert. It's no longer a dream, but a new reality. Carrie Underwood has achieved superstar status!

The Sky's the Limit

For many aspiring singers, the road to stardom is long and hard. Skill isn't always enough. Today's superstars need the whole package to make it in the music business. They need talent, **perseverance**, confidence, and stage-presence. Carrie Underwood has all of these and more. She is an award-winning recording artist who doesn't show any signs of slowing down!

Carrie performs for fans at Key Arena in Seattle, WA, during her Blown Away Tour on October 6, 2012.

4

Winning Ways

Carrie Underwood rocketed to fame after winning a singing competition on the hit talent show *American Idol*. The shy, **amateur** singer had no idea that she would beat thousands of other contestants for the title of American Idol. She simply amazed everyone with her beautiful voice and her dynamic smile.

Top-Notch

Carrie has had incredible success in the music industry in a very short time. Many of her songs have topped the Billboard Charts and won her some of the most **prestigious** awards in the music industry. Since 2005, this dedicated and hard–working artist has become one of the most famous country music singers the world has ever known.

It takes most singers years or even decades to win the awards Carrie has already won.

A Star Is Born

On March 10, 1983, Carole and Stephen welcomed a third daughter to the Underwood family. Carrie Marie Underwood was born in Muskogee, Oklahoma, and raised on a cattle farm in a small town called Checotah. Carrie's sister Shanna was 13 years old when Carrie was born, and her other sister Stephanie was 10 years old. Growing up, Carrie was very close to her family, and she still is to this day.

SWEET HOME CHECOTAH

Family is very important to Carrie. When she was on *American Idol,* she called her family every day just to be comforted by the sound of their voices.

On Another Path

Carrie's mother was a fifth grade teacher. Her father became a cattle farmer after working in a mill for 30 years. Carrie's sisters followed in their mother's footsteps and became teachers, too. But Carrie had different plans—she was determined to be a famous singer!

Shown here posing with her parents, Carrie has said that she started her life with the best family in the world already waiting for her!

6

Choir Practice

Carrie and her family attended the First Freewill Baptist Church every Sunday. As part of the church choir, Carrie got her first real taste of performing music, and she loved singing for an audience. She also sang in festivals and entered local talent contests to get more experience in front of a crowd. One of her teachers commented that when Carrie sang, she had stars in her eyes and a belief in herself.

Missed Opportunity

When Carrie was just 13, she was such a good singer that Capitol Records considered offering Carrie a recording contract. The deal never happened, however, due to changes at the record company. Carrie was extremely disappointed. She later realized that at 13, she really wasn't ready as an artist, and she counted that rejection as a blessing in disguise. She still had a lot of growing up to do!

Carrie learned to play piano and guitar at a young age.

For the Love of Animals

Growing up on a farm gave Carrie many opportunities to connect with nature. Her mom said that Carrie loved animals so much, she would even play with worms and snakes. At the age of 13, Carrie decided to stop eating meat because of her love and respect for animals. Her parents supported her decision, even though they raised beef cattle on their farm! Carrie is now a vegan, meaning she does not eat animal products of any kind, including eggs and dairy.

THE VOTES ARE IN!

In 2005, Carrie was voted "World's Sexiest Vegetarian" by animal-rights organization PETA.

Carrie's love for animals still shows as she teams up with Pedigree® to promote their Adoption Drive at the Bideawee Manhattan Shelter in New York.

Team Player

Carrie decided to pursue other interests while attending Checotah High School. Even though music was a big part of her life, she also enjoyed sports. Carrie joined the basketball and softball teams as well as the cheerleading squad. She didn't let these activities interfere with schoolwork, however, and she graduated second in her class in 2001.

Carrie used her softball skills at the City of Hope Charity Softball Game in Nashville Tennessee.

A Fork in the Road

After high school, Carrie decided to put her dream of becoming a singer aside and focus on continuing her education. She enrolled in a Mass Communications program at Northeastern State University to become a television news reporter. While education was important to her, Carrie's friends knew that music was in her blood. In 2004, Carrie's friends urged her to **audition** for the fourth season of *American Idol*. This push was what started Carrie on the path to superstardom!

The Road to Stardom

Starting in August 2004, over 100,000 people auditioned in seven cities across the United States in hopes of becoming the next American Idol. Carrie had the same goal as she drove with her mom and friend to St. Louis, Missouri, to audition.

The Chosen Ones

Carrie made it through the first round of auditions and was given the chance to perform for the *Idol* judges—Randy Jackson, Paula Abdul, and Simon Cowell. Her performance of Bonnie Raitt's hit song, "I Can't Make You Love Me" earned Carrie a golden ticket to perform in the next round of the competition in Hollywood, California. One hundred and ninety-two other contestants across the seven cities joined Carrie in the Hollywood rounds.

The harshest *American Idol* judge, Simon Cowell (right), predicted Carrie would win the contest and sell more records than anyone in *American Idol* history. So far he's right!

Whirlwind

When Carrie arrived in Hollywood, the competition was intense. The first round of solo performances eliminated 96 contestants. Next, after the group performances round, only 75 contestants were left. Another solo round eliminated 31 people. It was then down to just 44 contestants. Singing the song "Young Hearts Run Free" by Candi Staton, Carrie was chosen by the judges as one of the top 24 to move on to the semi-finals. There were 12 male and 12 female semi-finalists. From each group, two contestants were voted off the show each week by the judges.

SHE FORGOT!

During the Hollywood rounds, Carrie forgot the lyrics in her performance of "Young Hearts Run Free" by Candi Staton.

Carrie poses with the other contestants who were part of *American Idol's* Top 12 Women in 2005.

School's Out

To continue in the competition, Carrie had to commit to living in Hollywood. It was a hard decision, but she decided to put her final year at university on hold for a few months and follow her dream in Hollywood.

Home, Sweet Home

Throughout the semi-finals, Carrie was a fan favorite every week! She was overjoyed when she finally advanced to the Top 3, alongside Vonzell Solomon and Bo Bice. At this stage in the competition, the 3 finalists went back to their hometowns for a visit. When Carrie returned to Checotah, there were more than 10,000 people waiting to wish her good luck in the finals. The hometown visit included a parade for Carrie where people lined the street to wave, cheer, and take pictures of their hometown hero.

The Top 3 finalists perform together during the fourth season of *American Idol*.

She Said It

"Everyone here is so wonderful and I love this place, but I have to get back to work!"
—During the filming of her hometown visit for *American Idol*

It Takes Two

Back in Hollywood, the final three contestants performed three songs each. After the votes were counted, the person with the lowest number of votes was Vonzell Solomon. Carrie Underwood was in the Top 2, meaning she would compete against rocker Bo Bice for the title of American Idol. Both singers had tons of fans, so the pressure was on!

Tough Competition

Carrie's first performance was the song "Inside Your Heaven" by Desmond Child. The song was chosen by *American Idol* to be the winner's **anthem**. The winner would record and release the song as his or her first single. The second song Carrie chose to sing was a song from her musical influence Martina McBride, called "Independence Day." The song brought her good luck earlier in the competition, and she hoped it would do the same that night. Finally, she sang a song by Guy Sebastian, the winner of *Australian Idol*, 2003, called "Angels Brought Me Here."

After she performed her final song, Randy Jackson gave Carrie a **standing ovation**—the first one he'd given since the beginning of the competition!

The Winner's Circle

On May 25, 2005, more than 37 million votes were counted, and a winner was announced by *American Idol* host Ryan Seacrest. The talented Carrie Underwood from small-town Oklahoma had achieved her dream. She became the fourth *American Idol* champion, and the very first country singer to win. Carrie received a recording contract worth one million dollars with Arista Records. She also won a Ford Mustang Convertible and unlimited use of a private jet!

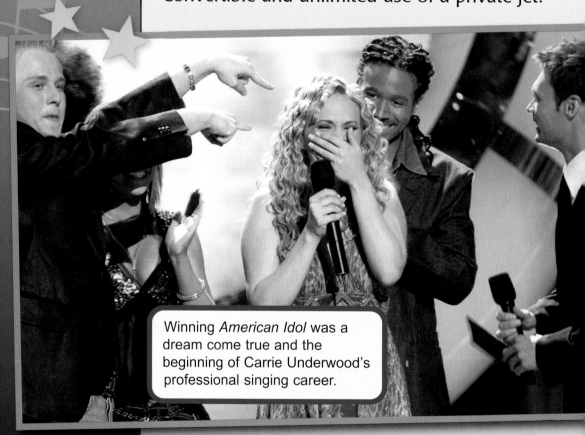

Winning *American Idol* was a dream come true and the beginning of Carrie Underwood's professional singing career.

She Said It

"All of this has been a great experience and I thank the American public so much for putting me in this position. I appreciate every second of it."
—In an interview with Billboard.com, June 2005

Shockwave

Carrie Underwood was in shock—she was the winner of *American Idol*! Just months before she won, she had been a senior in university with very different future plans. Naturally, the sudden adjustment to superstar status was exhausting. Carrie was kept busy doing appearances on several talk shows, such as the *Ellen Degeneres Show* and *The Tonight Show with Jay Leno*.

Life Is Grand

The most incredible invitation Carrie received after winning *American Idol* was to perform at the Grand Ole Opry in Nashville, Tennessee. Since 1925, the live-radio program has brought country music to people all over the world. Carrie always dreamed of performing on the Opry stage and, on June 10, 2005, she got her wish!

JOIN THE CLUB

On May 10, 2008, Carrie became the youngest member of the Grand Ole Opry at the age of 26. She was officially welcomed by long-time member and country superstar, Garth Brooks.

Carrie makes her **debut** performance at the Grand Ole Opry in 2005.

15

Idol on Tour

The *American Idol* Season Four Summer Concert Tour was Carrie's first experience performing on the road. During the summer of 2005, the Top 10 *American Idol* contestants traveled all over the United States and Canada performing concerts for fans. In all, the Idols performed 44 concerts between July and September of 2005.

IDOLS GIVE BACK

The Idols raised over 17 million dollars during their tour in support of "Idol Gives Back." The charity provides support and assistance to needy children in the United States and across the globe.

The Top 10 contestants join voices during the American Idols Live Tour in Sunrise, Florida, on July 12, 2005.

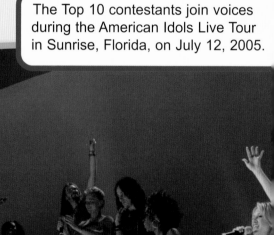

Some Hearts

There was never a dull moment for Carrie. When she wasn't performing, she was working on her first album. She released two singles off the album in October 2005, called "Jesus, Take the Wheel" and "Some Hearts." Her album, also called *Some Hearts*, was officially released on November 15, 2005. Just over a year after its release, *Some Hearts* was named the number-one selling album of the year at the Billboard Music Awards. It also set a record for being the best-selling debut album of any female country music artist in history.

Promotional posters for Carrie's debut album, *Some Hearts*, hangs in an Oklahoma City record store.

She Said It

"Carrie Underwood's debut album (has)...a country feel with some pop added to it. Lots of variety in her vocals, which tells me she has true talent."
—Penny Rondinella, reviewing Carrie's debut album *Some Hearts* for www.About.com

Graduation

In between photo shoots, TV and radio shows, touring, and working on her album, Carrie also made time to finish her last three months of school. She graduated from Northeastern State University on May 6, 2006, with a bachelor's degree in Mass Communications.

Carrie proudly walks the stage during her graduation ceremony at Northeastern State University.

The Crossover

In August 2006, Carrie released the single "Before He Cheats." This song was different than her last two country hit singles. This song was her first **crossover** hit—a mix of country and rock—and the lyrics took some people by surprise. Carrie's wholesome, tender-hearted personality had always been mirrored in her song lyrics. But this song's lyrics focused on getting **revenge** by destroying someone's property! Carrie has made it known to fans that she doesn't agree with this, she states "it's just a song!"

Carrie performed her single "Before He Cheats" at the 2007 CMT Music Awards.

She Said It

"It's great when you can write a meaningful song that touches people, but sometimes you just wanna have fun and sing a silly song that doesn't reflect on you as a person."
—In an article by Michelle Tauber on www.people.com

Roller Coaster Ride

Carrie's second album *Carnival Ride* was released on October 23, 2007. It sold over 2 million copies in just two months, and rode to Number 1 on the Billboard Chart and the Canadian Albums Chart. Carrie received Grammys for two singles on the album: "Last Name" and "I Told You So." Carrie had four number-one hits on *Carnival Ride*, making her the first female solo artist to do so since Shania Twain in 1998.

On Tour

After the release of *Carnival Ride*, Carrie joined forces with another famous country star, Keith Urban. Their tour was called "Love, Pain, and the Whole Crazy Carnival Ride." They visited 24 cities together. The tour ran from January through April of 2008. Carrie also headlined her own Carnival Ride Tour playing to more than a million fans in 105 cities.

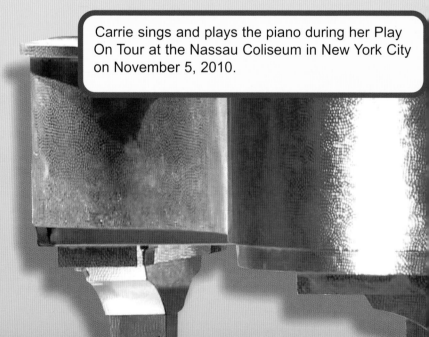

Carrie sings and plays the piano during her Play On Tour at the Nassau Coliseum in New York City on November 5, 2010.

Carrie On!

On November 3, 2009, Carrie released her third album entitled *Play On*. It was the second top-selling release by a female artist for the year 2009. Her hit "Cowboy Casanova" jumped to number one on Billboard's Hot Country Songs chart after just 10 weeks.

Change for Change

Carrie's Play On Tour began on March 11, 2010, and finished on January 1, 2011. The single "Change" inspired Carrie to donate 36 cents for every ticket purchased to the Save the Children fund to improve and support the lives of children around the world. She played 109 shows to over a million fans across North America, making it her biggest tour yet.

The Dream Continues

ACE IS WILD!

Carrie's dog, a rat terrier named Ace, was dressed in a pink tuxedo at the wedding!

Backstage after one of her concerts, Carrie met her future husband, a Canadian National Hockey League (NHL) player named Mike Fisher. Introduced by a common friend, they soon began dating. Mike played for the Ottawa Senators NHL team and Carrie had a busy schedule touring, so it was difficult to find time together as a couple. But they made it work, and on December 20, 2009, Mike proposed to Carrie and she said yes!

Here Comes the Bride

Carrie and Mike were married at the Ritz-Carlton Lodge in Greensboro, Georgia, on July 10, 2010, in front of more than 250 friends and family members. They share a strong **Christian** faith, and their wedding ceremony included readings from the Bible and a special performance of their favorite song, "Love Never Fails" by Brandon Heath.

Carrie and Mike support one another in their chosen careers, as shown here during the Billboard Music Awards in 2012.

Animal Care

Carrie shows her love for animals in significant ways. Carrie created the Checotah Animal, Town, and School Foundation to give back to her hometown community. In April of 2011, she opened a shelter in her hometown called Happy Paws Animal Shelter. Many rescued animals have been placed in loving homes as a result. She has also performed Public Service Announcements "(PSAs)" speaking about her support of The Humane Society of the United States.

People Person

People are also a **priority** for Carrie. She is actively involved in a number of charitable organizations. Carrie has participated in a campaign started by *American Idol*, called Idol Gives Back, that helps children in Africa and the United States who live in poverty. She also recorded a song called "Just Stand Up!" along with other artists, to raise millions of dollars for the charity "Stand Up to Cancer."

Carrie is pictured at the fundraising concert for the 2010 Idol Gives Back **campaign,** which raised over 45 million dollars in donations.

Branching Out

Singing isn't Carrie Underwood's only talent. When she was younger, she was an actress in many school musicals. In 2011, Carrie landed her first major-motion picture role in the movie *Soul Surfer*, a story about a surfer named Bethany Hamilton who lost her arm in a shark attack when she was only 13 years old. Carrie played Sarah Hill, a church youth leader who helps Bethany make sense of her life after the attack. Carrie has also performed on television shows including *How I Met Your Mother* and *SNL* (*Saturday Night Live*).

Carrie makes her acting debut, playing the roll of Sarah Hill in *Soul Surfer*.

She Said It

"*I feel like on the set, everyone was so nice and they helped me out so much. They were very patient with me and very understanding that this was my first movie. Onstage I know what to do, but in front of the lights and being on the movie set, I was pretty lost most of the time.*" —Discussing *Soul Surfer* in an article online by Kara Warner, www.mtv.com, April 7, 2011

Blown Away

Blown Away is Carrie's fourth album, released on May 1, 2012. It went to number one on the Billboard 200 Chart, and stayed there for more than two weeks—longer than any of her other albums. The Blown Away Tour was Carrie's first international tour. She played 105 cities in North America, 5 cities in Europe, and 4 in Australia. The tour began on May 26, 2012, and ran until June 30, 2013.

Around the World

With the release of each of her albums, Carrie Underwood has toured far and wide to bring her music to her fans. She completed five tours in six years. During her Blown Away Tour, Carrie and her band visited three continents and six countries. They played for more than a million fans at 112 concerts. To transport her crew, set, and equipment, it required nine tour buses and 16 trucks!

The Blown Away Tour was Carrie's longest tour to date, lasting more than a year.

Reaching Out

Carrie Underwood's unbelievable success has not changed the person she has always been. From an early age, her **compassion** and kindness toward others fueled her desire to help those in need. Recently, part of her home state of Oklahoma was destroyed by devastating tornadoes. Several families lost their loved ones, and many more lost homes and businesses. Carrie **pledged** an incredible amount of money from her Blown Away Tour—one million dollars— to the American Red Cross.

On May 20, 2013, a tornado cut a path of destruction more than 9 miles (14.5 km) wide in Moore, Oklahoma.

She Said It

"I have watched the devastation in my home state of Oklahoma over the past several days with great sadness. With the help of my fans who attended my concerts over the past year, we can offer the Red Cross a little extra help in comforting those affected by the recent tornadoes."

—In an article by Sherry Rickmaier, online, May 201

Award Winner

Each year the National Academy of Recording Arts and Sciences gives out awards of excellence to those in the recording industry. The Grammy Awards are the highest honor for a recording artist in any music **genre**. Carrie Underwood has won six Grammy Awards, including Best New Artist, Best Female Vocal Performance, and Best Country Song. She has also won awards in other countries, including Australia, France, and Great Britain. In all, she has won 118 awards from across the globe!

A Little Bit Country

Even though she is considered a country artist, her music has received **airplay** on radio stations that specialize in rock, pop, and adult contemporary. Carrie is a **versatile** artist, but her heart is in country music. Since 2005, she has been nominated for 23 Academy of Country Music Awards. The hard-working singer won 10 of those awards, including two awards for Entertainer of the Year.

Winners at the American Country Awards are awarded custom-made guitars instead of trophies. Carrie is the all-time top winner with 11, winning 6 of them in 2010.

Play On!

Like the title of her third album, Carrie Underwood plans to continue singing and acting for a long time. Recently, she signed on to play the role of Maria in a made-for-television version of Rodgers and Hammerstein's musical *The Sound of Music*. NBC will air the live performance on TV in December 2013. Carrie plays a young woman who becomes **governess** to a family of seven young children in Austria during the time of World War II.

FOOTBALL FAN

Carrie is the new performer of the *Sunday Night Football* theme song, "Waiting All Day for Sunday Night." Her song debuted during the September 8, 2013, game between the Dallas Cowboys and the New York Giants.

Ride On!

Carrie's life has been a roller-coaster ride of experiences since the moment she was crowned winner of *American Idol*. She has sold over 15 million albums and her songs have been number-one hits 17 times. There's no doubt this dynamic performer's career will continue to twist, turn, and entertain, just like an exciting Carnival Ride!

Carrie took over from musician Faith Hill as the performer of the famous *Sunday Night Football* theme song.

Timeline

1983: Carrie Marie Underwood is born on March 10 in Muskogee, Oklahoma

1996: Capitol Records offers a recording contract, but the deal falls through

2001: Graduates from Checotah High School with the second-highest marks

2001: Enrolls in the Mass Communications program at Northeastern State University

2004: Decides to audition for *American Idol*

2005: Wins the fourth season of *American Idol* on May 25

2005: Goes on tour with Top 10 contestants of *American Idol*

2005: First album *Some Hearts* is released on November 15

2006: Graduates from the Mass Communications program at Northeastern State University

2007: Releases her second album, *Carnival Ride*

2007: Travels to South Africa for "Idol Gives Back"

2008: Becomes the youngest member of the Grand Ole Opry on May 10 at age 26

2009: Releases her third album, *Play On*

2010: Marries NHL player Mike Fisher on July 10

2011: Plays the role of Sarah Hill in the movie *Soul Surfer*

2012: Releases her fourth album, *Blown Away*

2012: Sings the National Anthem at *Superbowl XLIV*

2013: Reaches out to tornado victims in Oklahoma City through a donation to the American Red Cross

2013: Becomes the new performer of the *Sunday Night Football* theme

2013: Signs on to play the role of Maria in the made-for-television muscial *The Sound of Music*

Glossary

airplay When a song is played on the radio

amateur Not yet a professional

anthem A song used repeatedly to represent the importance and celebration of an event or country

audition When a performer tries out for a show or performance

campaign A purposeful series of activities to achieve a goal

Christian A person who has faith in Jesus Christ

compassion Caring about the well-being of others

crossover An artist's change from one genre of music to another

debut The first time a song, album, or performance is delivered

genre Different styles of music, such as country, rock, pop

governess A woman employed to look after and teach children in their home

perseverance Steadily sticking to a course of action

pledged Promised or committed

prestigious Highly-regarded, top-notch

priority Item of importance

revenge The act of getting back at others for being wronged

standing ovation Applause that is given while standing

versatile Having the ability to do many different things well

XLIV Roman numeral for the number 44

Find Out More

Books

La Bella, Laura. *Carrie Underwood* (Who's Your Idol?). New York: The Rosen Publishing Group, 2008.

Tieck, Sarah. *Carrie Underwood* (American Idol Winner). Minnesota: ABDO Publishing Company, 2009.

Tracy, Kathleen. *Carrie Underwood*. Hockessin, Delaware: Mitchell Lane Publishers, 2006.

Websites

Carrie Underwood Online
www.carrieunderwoodofficial.com
Carrie's official website

Bio.True Story
www.biography.com/people/carrie-underwood-16730308
A biography of Carrie Underwood's life

American Idol
www.americanidol.com
The official site of *American Idol*

Twitter

https://twitter.com/carrieunderwood

Index

About the Author

Kylie Burns is a part-time freelance writer and a full-time teacher. She has written children's books on a variety of cool topics. She feels grateful to teach children all day—then write for them at night. At home, she has three great kids, a supportive husband, and one very demanding guinea pig.